The End of Love

Prose Poems by John Clark Vincent

Copyright © 2020 by John Clark Vincent. All rights reserved. No part of this publication may be reproduced or transmitted in any form or by any means, without permission in writing from the author.

Cover and interior design by Lisa D. Holmes (Yulan Studio, yulanstudio.com)

Published in Portland, Oregon by Yulan Studio, Inc.
Printed in the United States.

First edition
ISBN: 978-0-9915382-7-0

… for Lisa Dianna Holmes

Table of Contents

The Beauty in Goodbye 7
Soft as My Intention 9
It's the Darkness to Which I Cling 11
Falling Leaves of Spring 13
The Ache of Every Truth We Never Shared 15
Memorial to a Life I Can't Remember 17
The Sweet Stench of Kept Promises 19
Waiting for Help 21
With Completely Absent Minded Love 23
Descending as a Faded Memory 25
Rediscovering Love 27
The Children of Someone Else's Dream 29
Living Two Separate Lives 31
Letters from the Land of Stone 33
His Heart Weeps in All Weathers 35
As the Cool Porcelain Met Her Touch 37
The Piano Tuner and His Wife 39
A Jazzy Kind of Sorrow 41
The View at Twilight 43
Whispering the Promises of Love 45

The Beauty in Goodbye

Cold sneaks in everywhere when you're old. It doesn't so much engulf you... it just settles in. But it can also shake you awake. Like autumn reminds the leaves they still can sing when so little hope remains after summer's heat and such scant rain.

The sudden shiver in autumn's breath wakes them up again. Helps them recall all the hues they started with. All the colors they still carry on the inside when they let their guard down. When they're finally willing to stop trying so hard to be something more.

When they see the end approaching and begin to accept themselves as they are. We're like that, too, you know. Once we stop trying to grow, we start feeling more free to be who we always were meant to be.

I guess that could seem sort of sad... that we wait that long... put off our freedom till the end of our song. But that's how nature works. It doesn't show us the last stanza until we've finished the first. That's the gift it holds on to.

The secret it just won't tell until we're finally ready to let that cold settle. Not fight it, but rather ignite it with a bursting bundle of dreams it now seems we no longer need. When we're no longer greedy for life, and life's no longer greedy for us.

That's the beauty in goodbye. That's what freedom really means. When our perfect colors light up every scene, and our breath comes slow and easy. As we settle in with the cool air and begin, ever so softly, to truly sing.

Soft as My Intention

Years later, as I stand behind you and touch your head in the back, low, just above your neck, then move my fingers up into those silky baby-fine hairs, soft as my intention, I am reminded that our love was once an infant too.

That was the time of new ideas. When we tested our voices, grabbed for the choices we made, and wove the threads of our togetherness around us like a chrysalis of hope. But age affects all and now, years later, that chrysalis has worn thin.

It wasn't pain or strife or down-wind distractions that took off the sheen. It was repetition. Waking each morning and, without thinking, getting two bowls and two spoons. Putting the sugar in one cup before drinking from the other.

Even raku rubs smooth in time, but that doesn't mean we love it less. It means we love it like our own breath. Like the way each moment we rub up against, every single day, feels familiar, no matter how much it may have changed from the day before.

So now, years later, as I stand behind you and touch your head in the back, low, just above your neck, then move my fingers up into those silky baby-fine hairs, soft as my intention, I am reminded that our love was once an infant too.

It's the Darkness to Which I Cling

It is common for me to speak highly of the lighter parts of life. The sunny days. Times when people are kind to one another, and kittens have plenty of milk. But, truth be told, it's the darkness to which I cling. The secret, silent times.

Those are the moments when everything, finally, is simply perfectly still. And enveloped within that quiet, any hurt that's built beyond what I can further carry can be laid down, as the rawness fades to a throbbing memory of what I could no longer do.

For me, there is a softness to the dark. An acceptance I do not need to observe. A kindness I can't explain and, on truly rare occasions, the fading reflection of a far too cleverly hidden spark of hope. But, mostly, there is me. Reaching for nothing.

Simply lost in remembering the many faces of life and of love that led me here.

Falling Leaves of Spring

Back then, more than almost anything, it was her hands he was drawn to... slender palms and long, tapering fingers that reminded him of a colt's ungainly legs which somehow enabled it to run as smoothly as a breeze bends grass. They were artist's hands, molding her vision, bringing her spirit to life... and offering so much to him as well... confidence and comfort and an uncompromising sensuality. He would awaken to them brushing hair from his face, warm to them when she acknowledged him as she walked by, melt from them as they soothed his temples and neck, and reach for them when she needed reassurance.

For her, it was his mouth. The way it used words and performed other more intimate tasks. She loved the shape of his lips, their soft embrace. His was a poet's mouth that offered her songs she had never heard before he spoke them. She loved the easy way he laughed and the spontaneous fun to which that laughter often led. She loved to touch her lips to his each morning to renew the pool of affection they drifted in, as his fingers traced hers, fingertips touching as lips touch, urging the surge of life to engulf them. And engulf them it did.

Today, if pressed, they both will tell this same tale. Looking wistfully through a window at the fading bracts of dogwood blossoms, or absently staring into steam rising from a cup of Wuyi or Ti Kuan Yin. They both feel sure they have not left the paths that brought them together, and yet, together they are not, though neither knows exactly why that is. So I ask them if, perhaps, their paths were not running parallel after all, but instead were echoing the curve of discovery, merging ardently as crossing streams, then advancing with the pulse of desire. And that while drifting, they simply drifted apart.

She smiles at the notion... a small sad smile... then looks away. His expression does not change, and the steam continues to rise.

The Ache of Every Truth We Never Shared

Remember that summer when we were eleven and in love and your mother gave me her recipe for Sablé Breton? It was in her kitchen we gained our first glimpse of what love might be. Can you believe that now, forty years later, I still bake those cookies. I'm known for them.

But I am married and you are gay, and we both are turning grey. Yet, somehow, the taste of that time lives on in the butter and flour and heat and fragrance and every other part of our innocent endeavor... our small beginning which cannot seem to write an easy ending.

So I carry you, and the ache of every truth we never shared, to every party I attend. You're with me now, in fact, as I wait for friends who could not understand how hard it is to give you away again and again, each time thinking... maybe this time really is goodbye.

Then today you called to say hello. And I wanted to reach across time, take your floured hands in mine, and truly feel what it is to begin again. Though I know we never will. So I gather the crumbs of each evening's end, thank your mother for her kindness, and bid my friends adieu.

Memorial to a Life I Can't Remember

Rediscovering a long lost love on the internet is like tossing a baited hook into an isolated stretch of water once fruitful. Knowing this river was fished out years ago, but allowing the fantasy to swell with each deceptive tug of current.

I've fished this river so many years. Spent anxious times, alone moments, frightening instances of natural selection. But ultimately, I'm left wondering what might have come from so many small challenges to which I failed to rise.

They were not mistakes that were made. They were choices. Not failure to finish, but failure even to begin, coupled with a willingness to forgive myself too easily. Until forgiveness, piled upon forgiveness, fills the shopping cart I still mortgage.

Finally the rocks rub my bait away, as I discover the name that sparked this journey leads to little. An obituary. Memorial to a life which, mostly unknown to me, I can't remember and therefore cannot mourn.

The Sweet Stench of Kept Promises

The trail turned rough a few miles back. Stones lifted by patience, stoically rising from soil eroded through decades of makeshift riverbeds and too many hikers, awakened by light from every midday dawn, rise to meet my boots. This trail and those it carries descend to greet a creek, a salmon stream, clinging to its heritage with shallow songs now sharp, now softly sullen, now coursing on to larger tales than these.

Rounding a bend that forces my feet to water's edge I see this day's first chinook. Too large. Silvered back exposed, darkening with the need to spawn. Fighting a dearth of water more than any current, it has lived a life and now remembers the promise made amid these smooth pebbles. Let me live. Let me live and swim and feed freely, and the day will come when I repay the gift and dance once more along these banks.

Who hasn't felt this call of home, this will to arrive at meaning. A return to peace from life rash and clumsy, exhausting, yet eventually cherished as we sense the stream grow shallow. Sense, then feel, then see, then understand that we have grown too large to swim among these pebbled memories. Too tired to turn away. We swim where others have swum. We swim until we're greeted with the sweet stench of kept promises.

Waiting for Help

When he was young, there were moments when his father could not stand. Could only lay, back in spasm, rigid with pain, on vibrant teal carpet his mother had chosen for their dining room floor. His father would lay beside the used, upright piano his mother had found at a local sale, then painted pink once it was delivered. It was the piano he enjoyed playing but hated practicing on. He never practiced when his father's back was bad.

His father's fingers squeezed, white knuckled, anything in reach... a leg of the piano stool or even a pipe feeding the heat radiator if the spasms came in warmer months. Who knows why the piano stool wasn't pink. He always had assumed his mother ran out of paint, but he never asked her and now she's dead. So's his father, but he still remembers that one time the ambulance came.

A single tear rolled down his father's cheek as two attendants who knew him lifted him onto their gurney. It looked as though his father's fingers might snap that metal frame with his large hands, hardened by his farm and by his own stubbornness. He was afraid of his father, and he loved him. Before the ambulance arrived his older brother with some friends came by, back from college for a surprise visit.

His father made him meet them at the door and find a way to keep them outside. Don't let them in, his father insisted. So he took his own meager savings and gave it to his brother and sent the laughing group upon an errand. He doesn't remember what they bought, but he can't forget how proud he felt, even though his father said nothing. Because it wasn't praise he was looking for as they held hands, waiting for help.

With Completely Absent Minded Love

Every Thursday night they sit together in that same worn out pub. At the table in the back beside the portrait of a yellow Labrador retriever. I mean… it's not a photo. It's oil on canvas. And it's beautiful. The way only a dog who loves you can be beautiful… with unquestioned commitment and lots of accidents. Someone really must have loved that dog. Maybe they remember him… who knows why they sit there.

Tonight they're with another couple… friends perhaps. And looking on, one might wonder how such a lithe and animated woman like her could feel so at home with an old drunk like him. But she does. She engages and expresses and laughs and there… she touched him. As she spoke she touched him with completely absent minded love. I can feel the affection all the way over here. She ran her hand across his distended stomach with such tenderness.

It's as though she traced some journey they have shared. Some vague remembrance that lives on through the greasy food and the seasonal ale. Through the death of her mother, and the loss of their child. It's as though she's remembering the way he would pick her up when she had quit. The way he held her each time she fell. It's like she touched him knowing that should the days ahead turn dark like then, he would be there to pick her up again.

Descending as a Faded Memory

There is no record of the love we shared that one summer we were together, beyond a photograph I haven't been able to find for the past twelve years. It was a photo of the gabled house, nearly hidden by cedars, on the corner across from the room we shared while we waited for word about your future.

I guess I should say our future, which we both knew was ending. The question was simply how long... how much time did we have left? Oh we burned so brightly our one ill-fated summer. But I cannot help wondering... would the flames have raged within us regardless of what the future may have held?

Or was the promise of an ending the fuel for the bonfires that we built. Without that knowledge, would the moments we shared have engulfed us in such a way? Enabled us to gather our heat... the way the oceans gather heat... the way the air gathers heat.

Breathing it in, swimming in it, holding fast to one another and allowing it to consume us. Allowing it to burn away all the days we knew we would never see. Who could know the answer to a question like that. But I do know that even though our photo seems to have fled, our dust and our ash remain.

Rediscovering Love

Resolving to try, one last time, to find the love they somehow misplaced along the way, the two of them mingled all the thoughts they were willing to share. Then caught hold of each shard of memory that may have been chipped from what was once their dream.

They warmed those shards. Blowing hopeful, but, understandably, somewhat anxious breath upon them until they weren't so cold. And, eventually, the shards began to warm, and seemed nearly ready to actually glow.

So they whispered to those tiny possibilities of now hot hope how beautiful rebirth can be, until they began to sense that the growing embers were coming to understand how wonderful it is to be whole and to be free.

All the while, they pretended to be confident... each of them straining, secretly, to recognize their individual desires within these fledgling flames... then they stepped back, smiled nervously at one another, and waited for life to do whatever it decided to do.

The Children of Someone Else's Dream

This solstice feels darker than others I remember. It feels less certain. And somehow harder to breathe in and hold close. Harder to renew the hope that's seen me through so many darknesses, and allowed me to believe that I can actually do this thing called life. That I can survive in a world which appears incapable of love… indifferent to suffering… and, finally, this time, perhaps too sick to heal.

In fact, this solstice feels impossibly far from the seed stocks of real opportunity or the hapless wish for peace I've carried far too long. Still… I want to believe the light will come. I'm desperate for my heart to know that it will come. Maybe not now. Maybe not for us. But for the children of someone else's dream. And when it does, the light itself will know which paths to illuminate and which to leave alone.

Living Two Separate Lives

I mean, it felt weird, you know. The moment I realized the person I love is living her own life, not playing a part in mine. We're living two separate lives and weaving the edges of those lives together. We're creating a tapestry stretching from the moment we met to the day we finally forget each other.

Strangely, all this time I had thought of her as a major player in this comedy drama I attempt to star in and direct. So imagine my shock when I learned she's not co-starring in my play at all. She's running her own production. Which happens to be showing in the same theater I use all night and every day.

And when she speaks to me... when she shares her secrets and her dreams, if I listen, what I hear is the song of someone else's heart, not a harmony line to mine. It's been that way from the start. But the ear buds that I wear kept me focused on myself. Completely unaware of her sweet compositions.

I'll admit that since I made this discovery, I've wondered how many times I undercut her hopes or undervalued the gifts she's offered me. But more than anything, I'm doing my best to learn the notes she's writing and sense the key she's singing in so I can follow along and make our two songs harmonize.

Letters from the Land of Stone

One might expect that stones most admire stoicism and permanence. That they have no taste for news, and instead, each day, turn only to the long reads. That they seek the deeper visions, patiently pursuing their own small piece of eternity. And certainly, such suspicions are not without merit. Stones do all those things. But if you live among them, listen closely, and learn their language, the lyrics of their songs also tell a somewhat softer tale.

Because in fact, stones just love to immerse themselves in delicacy. They close their eyes as the grasses growing up around them bend before the wind to caress them again and again. Their judgements begin to relax as the morning sun opens her heart and pours her warmth upon them. And in those extra special moments when a butterfly alights on one to wile away some time, whether limestone, karst, or granite, that stone will smile and breathe, and oh so softly sigh.

For stones have the biggest hearts of all. Only an abundance of love can explain the willingness of stones to commit themselves for all of time to hold our world together. To give themselves pebble by pebble and grain by grain to the wind and rain and never ending tides of life that ask continually for some small piece of them. Something small enough to carry away. Something they can use to build a deeper connection to the foundation upon which we all depend.

His Heart Weeps in All Weathers

Sitting in an easy chair... preferably a big one. And old... worn into a comfortable form. Sitting... staring out the window, or at the corner of the ceiling, or into your eyes, anywhere. And always listening.

Listening to sad music. Sad for him at least. An adagio. A ballad. Some bit of neoclassical yearning. Ever a single breath away from tears. That was him at sixteen, and that is him today at sixty-eight.

Sober, drunk, high, in love, heartbroken, completely normal... it never has mattered what his condition was or is or may become. His heart weeps in all weathers. It's always prepared to breathe the music in.

Because it wants, so desperately, to leap into the very soul of love. To swim in that pond. To immerse itself in love's completely impossible dream. Then to rise, and find itself resting peacefully on the other side.

As the Cool Porcelain Met Her Touch

Her fingers were warmed by the teacup she held, and, honestly, that may have been her favorite part of drinking tea. On colder days she would grip the cup... no, not grip... grip is not the right word here. Let's say bundle... she would gently bundle her cup in both her hands just to pull the warmth she sought into her palms. Then she'd rest her open hand against her cheek. Oh, she just loved that sensation... couldn't keep her eyes open even if she had wanted to. Which she didn't and never would.

Some days, often the coldest part of the coldest days, she would lose herself in those cheek warming moments. Literally lose herself. The way an idea can just go away, completely unnoticed, and then be forgotten in a way that made it seem as though it never had existed in the first place. It was always her fingers that brought her back. They had grown cold while she was gone. And when she returned home... she liked to think of it as returning home when she came back... so when she returned home she would ease her fingers away from her cheek and press them lightly against her cup.

She knew there would not be sufficient heat remaining to rewarm them, but she didn't mind repeating the gesture each time that she returned. Perhaps it was out of respect to the tea and the cup which had done her such a good turn. Perhaps it was because she remained a hopeful person at heart. Or perhaps she simply found comfort in repetition. We each can choose our own way to see it. Regardless, she never failed to try, and each time, an almost smile appeared as the cool porcelain met her touch.

The Piano Tuner and His Wife

Finding, for the very first time, a lasting love with a kindred spirit during life's autumnal moments may be the most satisfying of all the ways people are joined together. At least, that's the way it appears for the piano tuner and his wife. The giddy anxiety he feels with each effort he makes to please her, and the peaceful joy she feels each time he succeeds is the stuff of dreams finally come true.

So when acquaintances, and even a few friends, have extended a bittersweet blessing by suggesting these melodic lovers were unfortunate to find one another nearer the end of their lives than the beginning, it may be that their thoughts are struggling with their own regrets, for their voices sound a bit off key. Because what could be more fortunate than knowingly living, heart aching with Spring's emerging joy, the nostalgic reality that many simply long for.

When asked how they came together, they speak of all the music they had heard and all the places they had traveled while alone. And they realized they were sharing, separately, the same music; the same countries. The same cities with the same cafés. Their entire lives had been in tune with one another. So they held each other's hand and continued to greet each morning with some berries and more than a little chocolate. But added, each evening, a tender kiss goodnight.

A Jazzy Kind of Sorrow

Hers is a jazzy kind of sorrow. A syncopated sadness that has slow danced around the edges of her long and, to be honest, quite varied life. What hasn't varied is how she has managed to live the majority of those years completely inside herself. Although, more recently, she has begun to give up her reticence to be seen. So each time she discovers herself standing just behind the edge of a window, leaning forward and intently peering out, she steps courageously right into open view and continues watching life unfold.

She understands that life is not passing her by. It is simply playing out in front of her, and she moves with it the same way she sways with ladybugs in her garden or juncos in the birdbath outside the window above her kitchen sink. In many ways it feels similar to… and this is a feeling she still remembers… it feels similar to standing at the edge of the dance floor watching her high school prom play itself out in the open spaces as she worked to take it all in. Trying to fathom what she might be missing. But she never came up with any answers.

Interestingly though, as her reticence to be seen began to ebb, so did any thought that anyone other than she should be deciding how her song is meant to be played. She knows how life works. She has studied it endlessly in great detail. And she has played her part as well as she was able. After all, not everyone is meant to improvise a solo. Most don't want to try. And some just love to watch and keep time. So now she regularly settles in, listens to sad, sensual jazz as loudly as she wants, and allows it to dance right in the center of her room.

The View at Twilight

Always, it seemed, there was some thing just out of reach. His entire life, it did not matter whether he was looking forward or back; another shoe, somewhere, might possibly drop; or some remedy he had concocted to resolve a past inadequacy still longed to be applied... if only he could get just one more chance to make his piece of this world right. And in doing so, to bring at least one small dream to life.

Hearing his story, one cannot help but wonder if the world he sought to modify, or to repair, lived only in his mind. That it wasn't real. And as he toiled with his heavy thoughts, the world that was real, comprising all the moments in his life, was ever so anxious for him to reach out to it, to watch it dance, caress its cheek, sit with it each evening, or wrestle it and help to make it strong. Make it feel as alive as it dreamed it could feel if only it was truly seen.

To his credit, although he longed for more, he never stopped building the foundations that might one day hold his dreams should they ever appear. Oh, there were detours, certainly... some quite long. But he held on. And, interestingly, the dreams seemed to hold to him as much as he held them. They wanted him. Needed him to help them step into the river and begin to swim. For they knew they never would arise if he did not help them make it so.

In the end, he never consciously chose to change his outlook. He still missed his keepsakes. But he did slow down. He slowed enough to notice how often his spaniel looked to him. How pretty maple leaves are when viewed against an autumn sky. Which flowers hummingbirds prefer in July. How deeply his wife loved him, and how she proved that love over and again. In truth, his twilight had arrived, and real life simply looked more dear within the changing light.

Whispering the Promises of Love

When I die, the lighter parts of me will fly. Some will soar like long held dreams that, finally, have been set free. The rest will drift… as clouds or incense drifts… floating in and out of life's ever shifting consciousness.

The heavier parts of me will embrace the earth. Maybe find old friends within the soil, or travel some previously unimagined path that leads to opportunities waiting just for me. And slowly begin to build a newer dream.

Regardless, all these parts that once were me will sense one another… recognize themselves as they pass by… singing the songs of every moment we've passed through, while whispering the promises of love that has not yet arrived.